When Love Happen

Valentine's Day Coloring Book

Your Love

Your Way

Just Color It

Anny Will

Happy Coloring

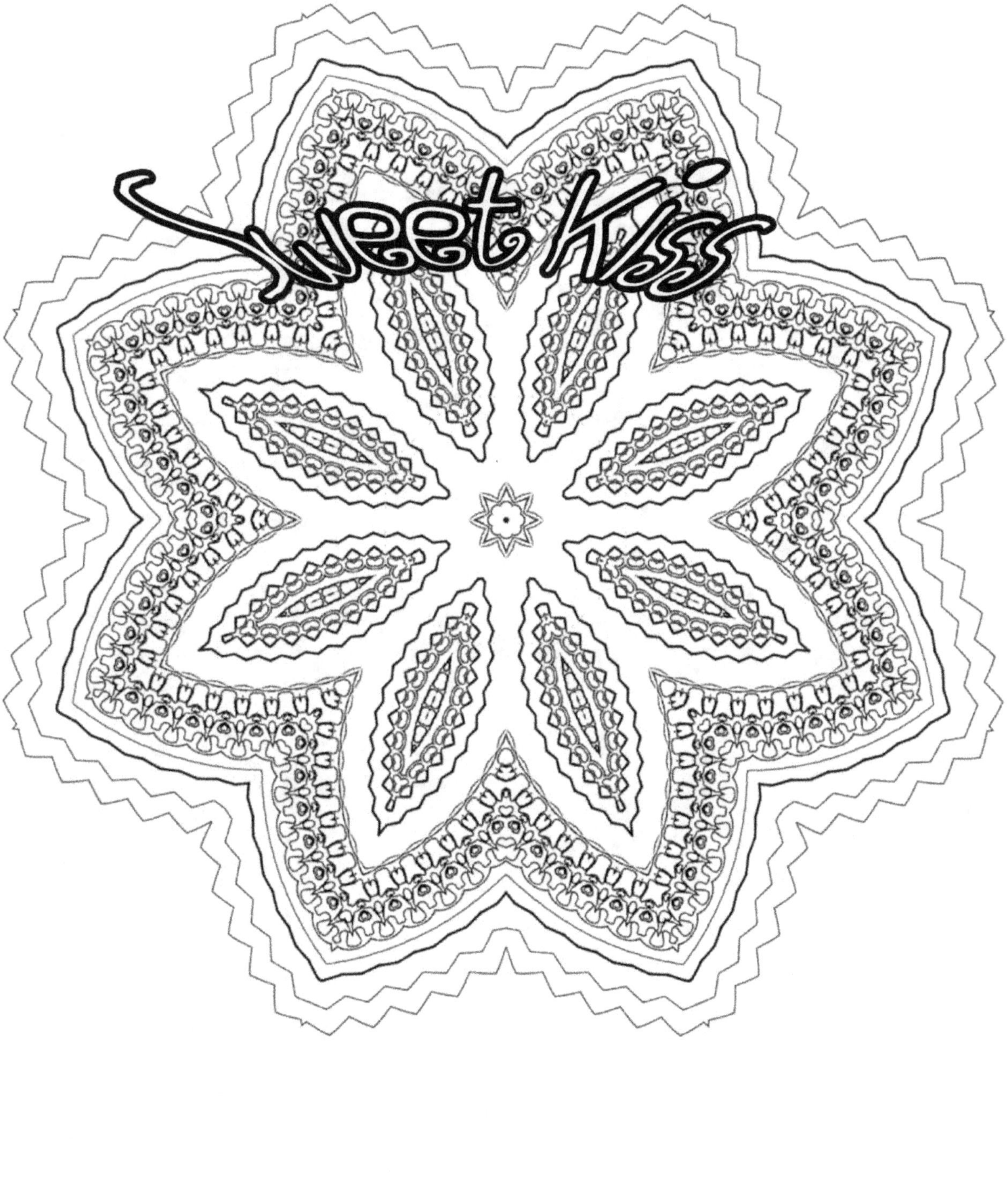
Sweet Kiss

Love in the Mist

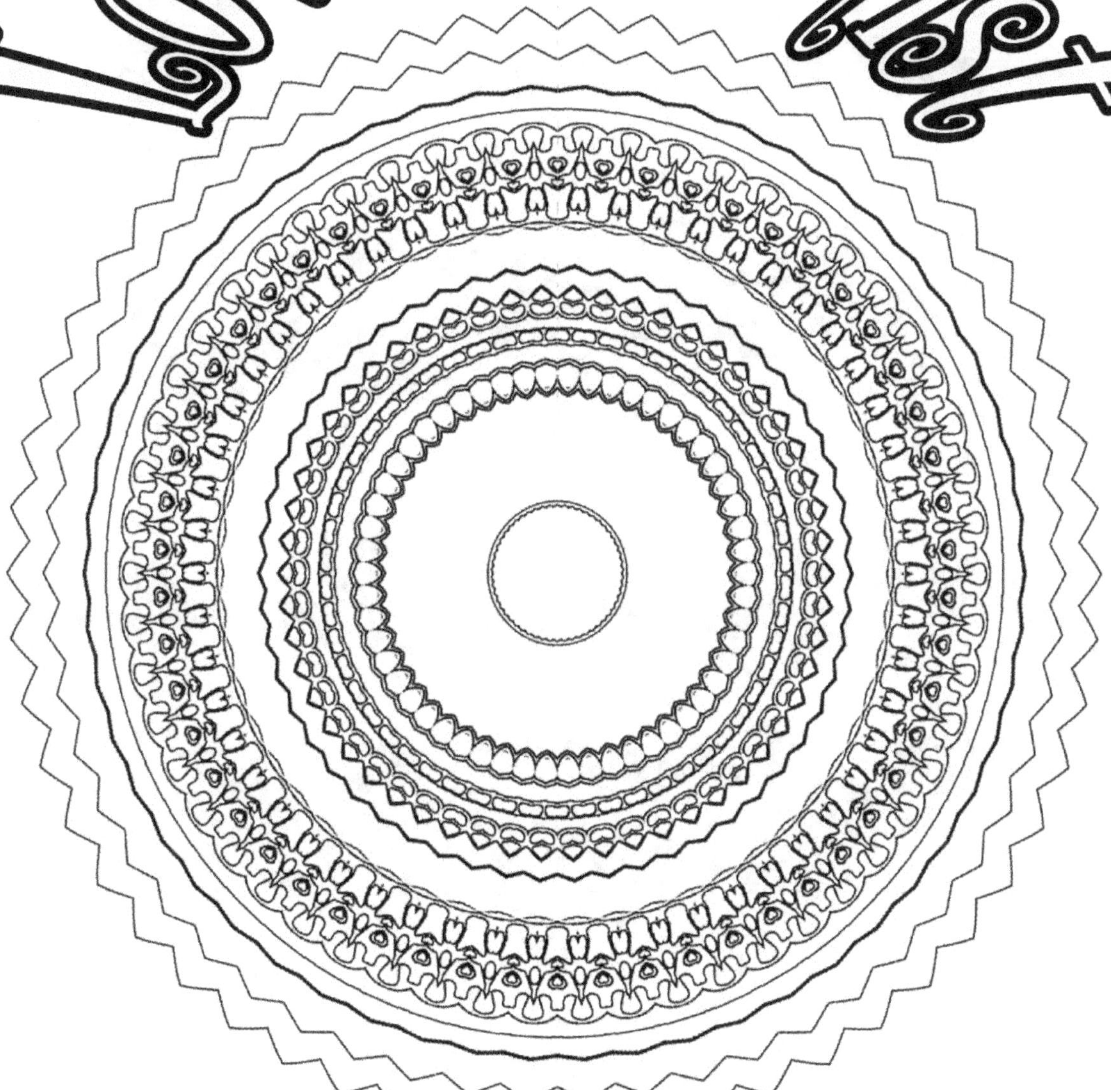

The Melody of Love

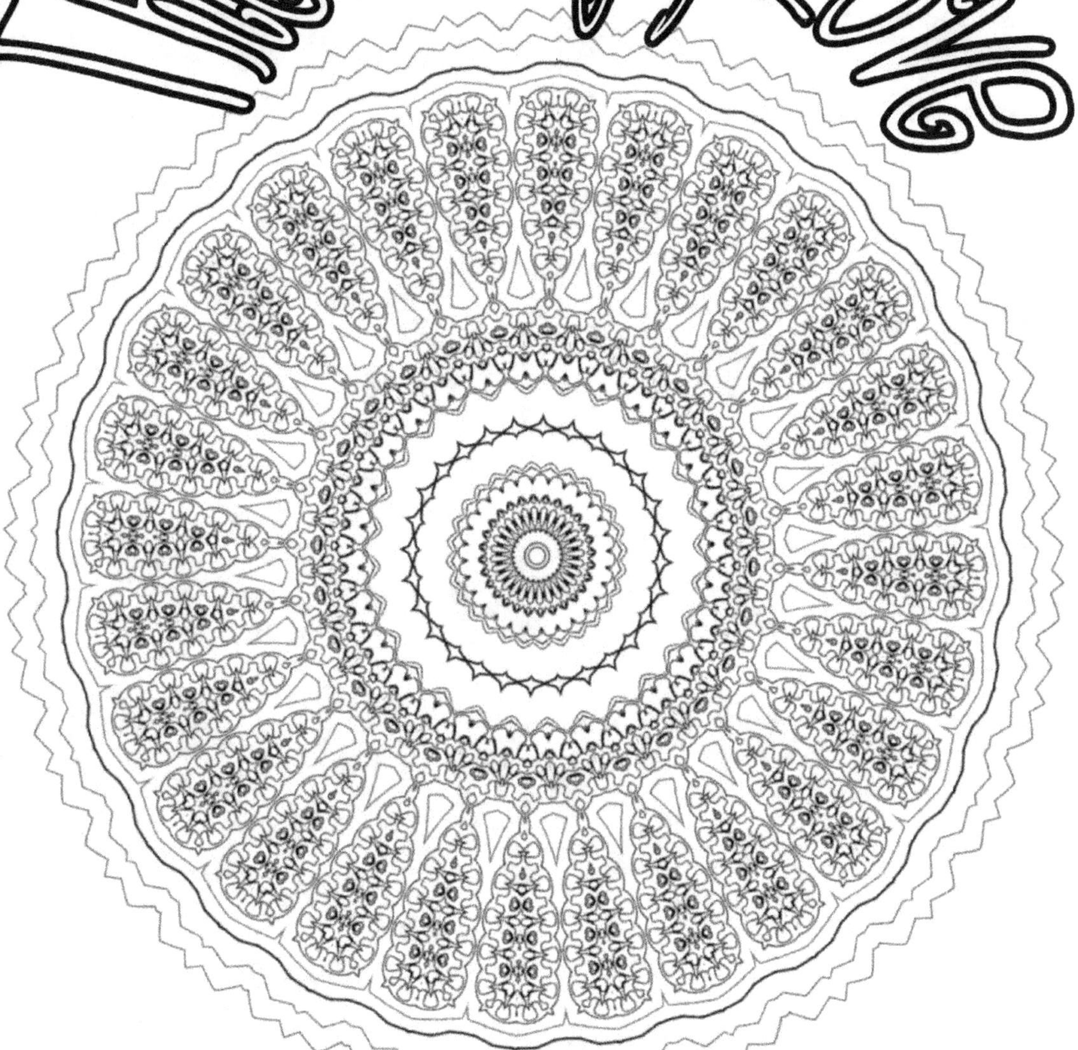

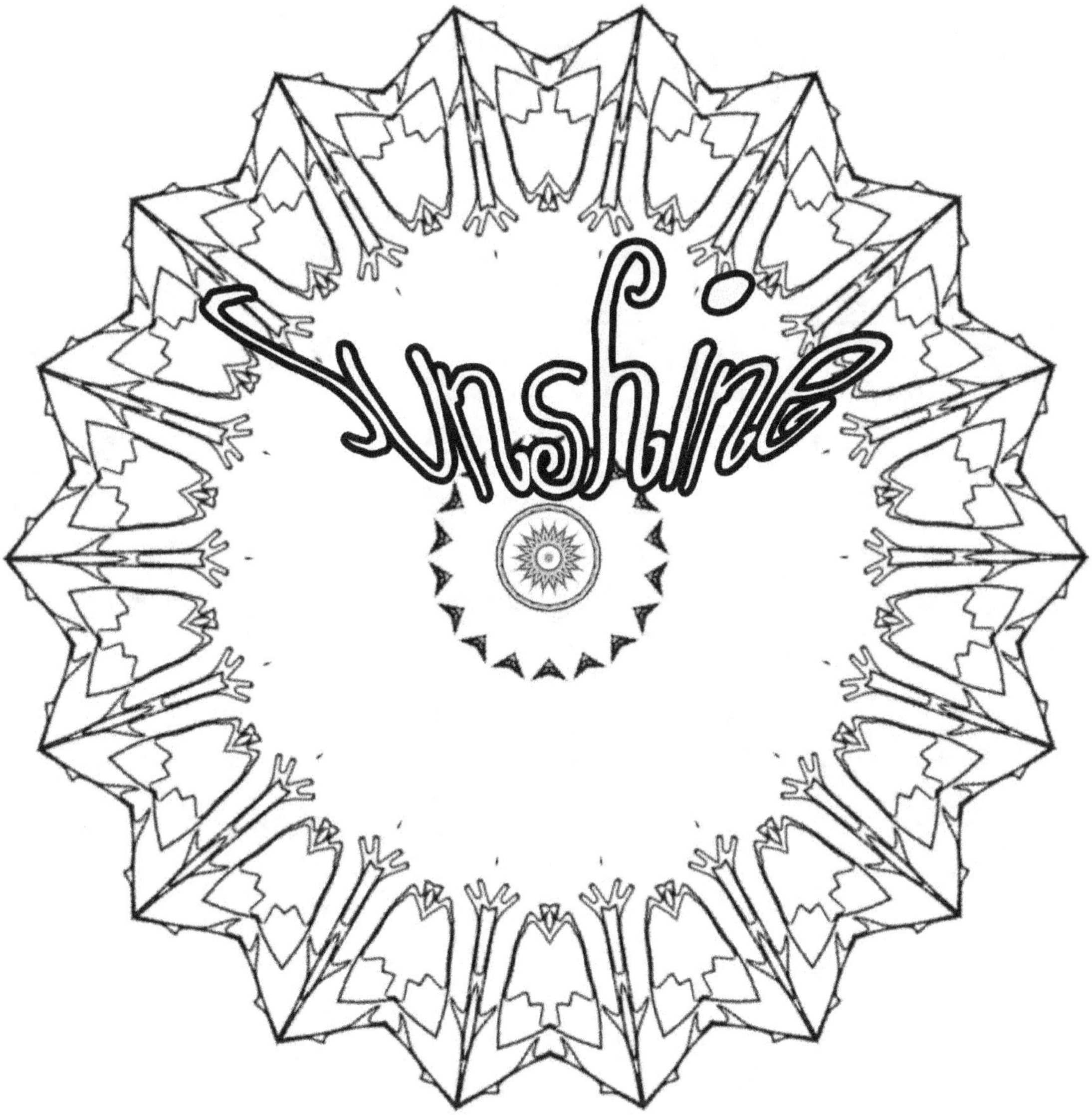
Sunshine

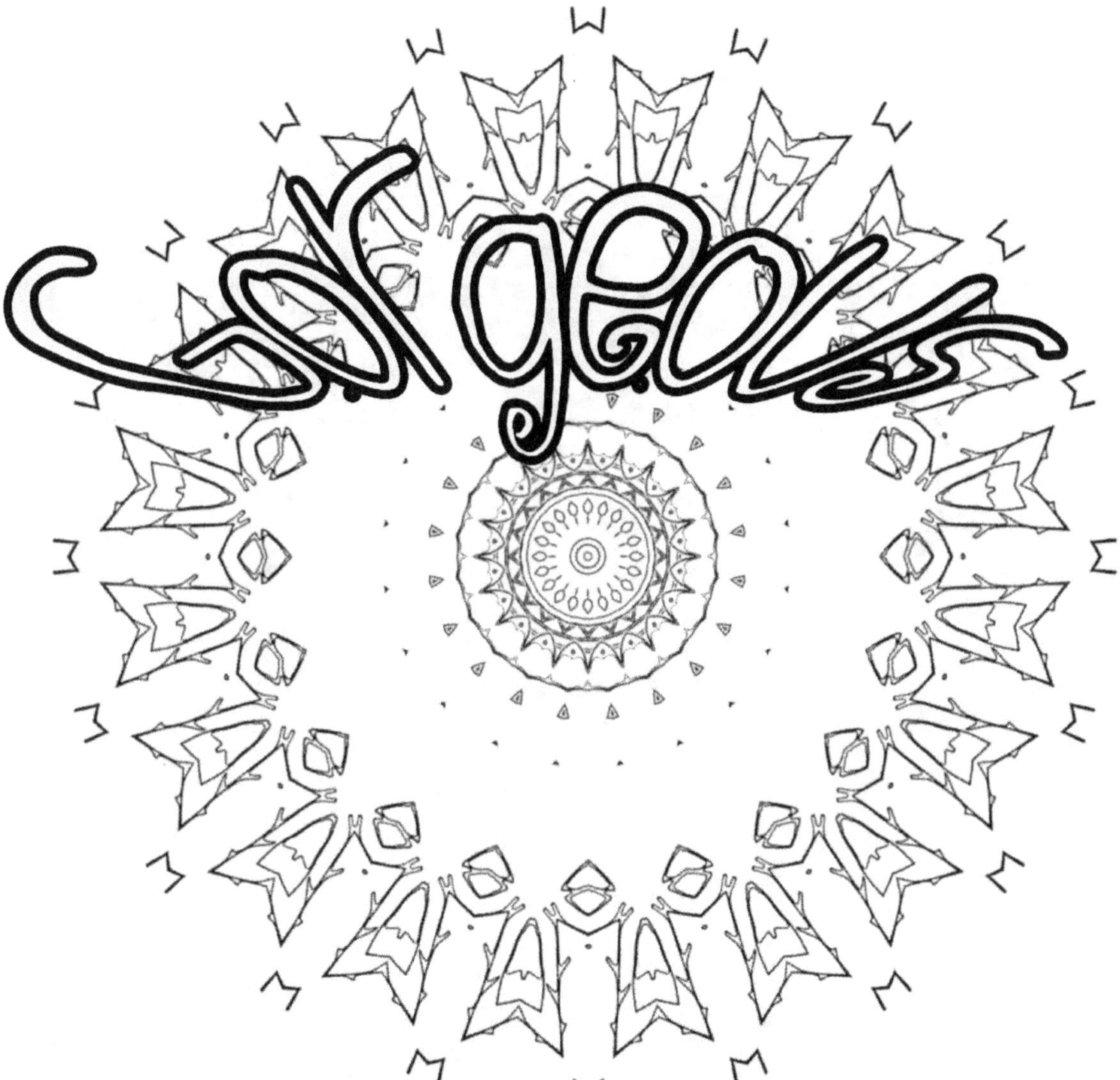

My Love

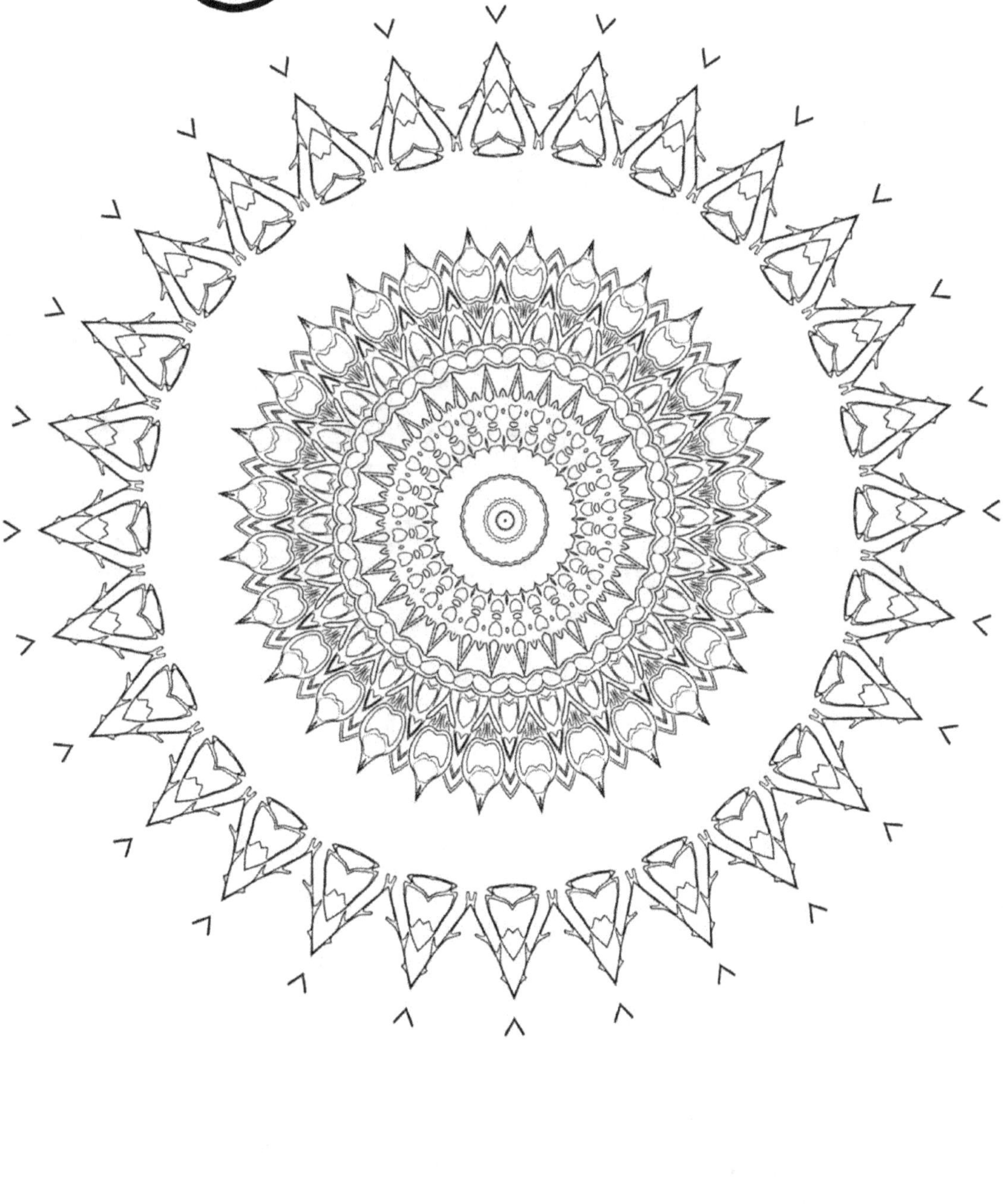

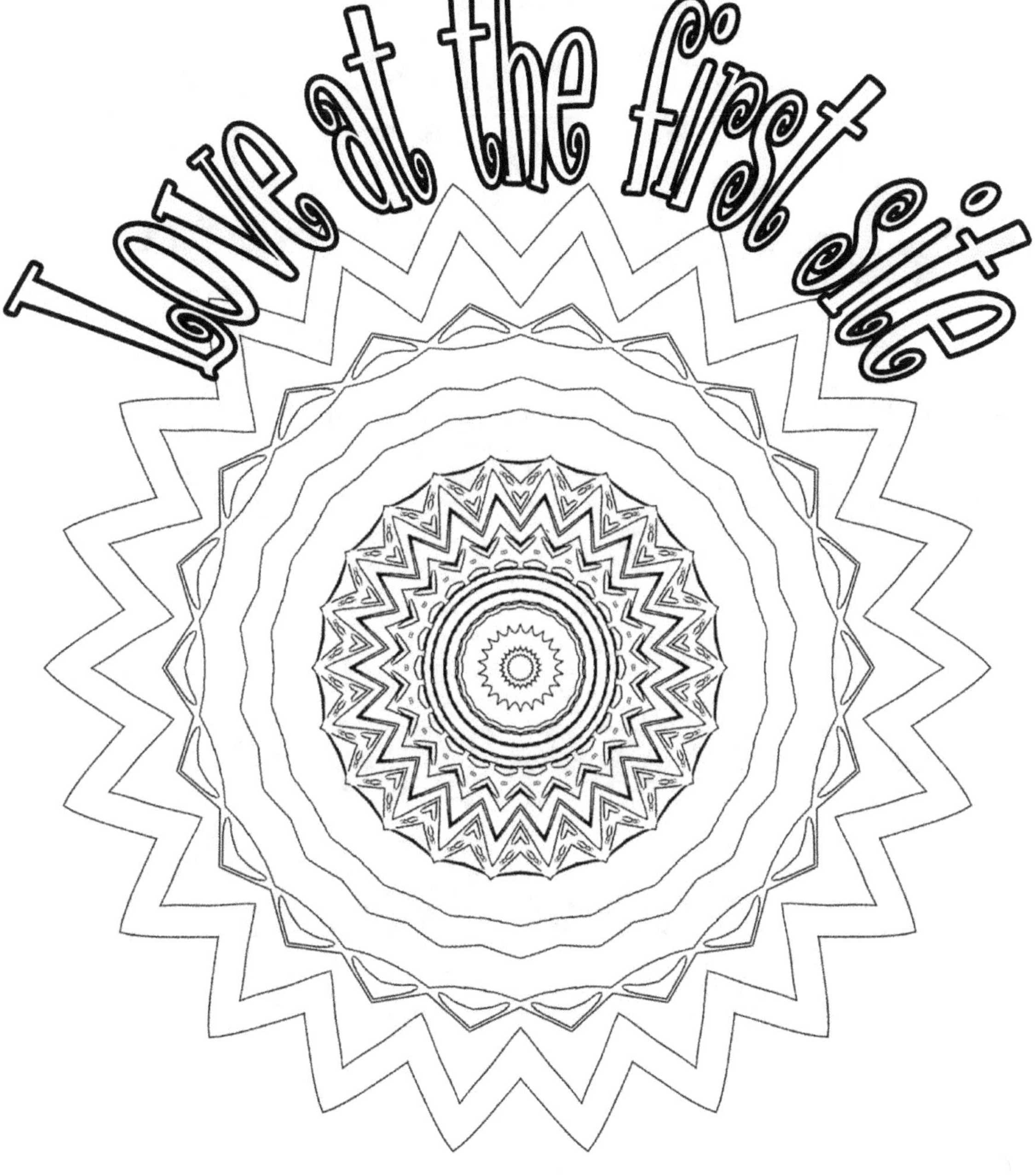
Love at the first site

A Cup Of Love

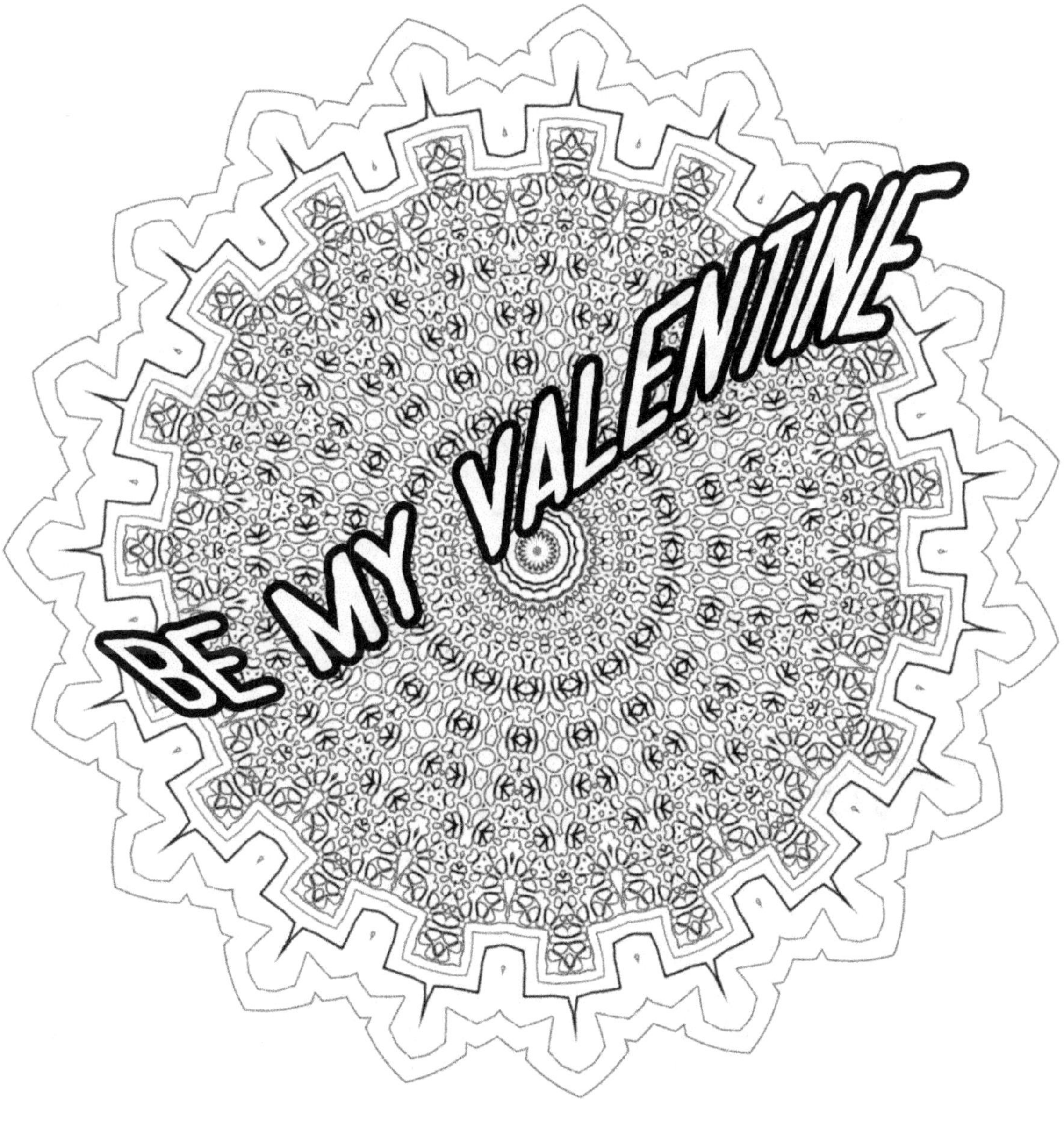
BE MY VALENTINE

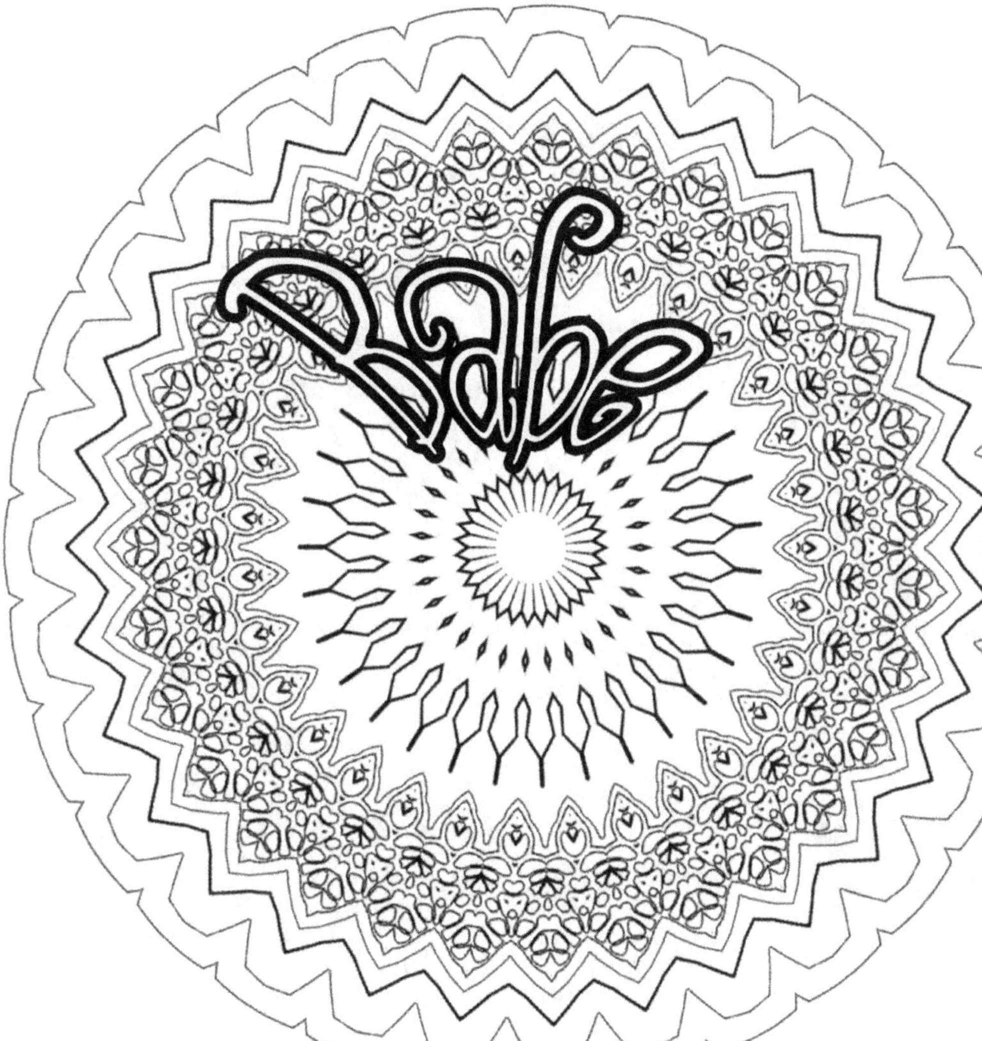
Babe

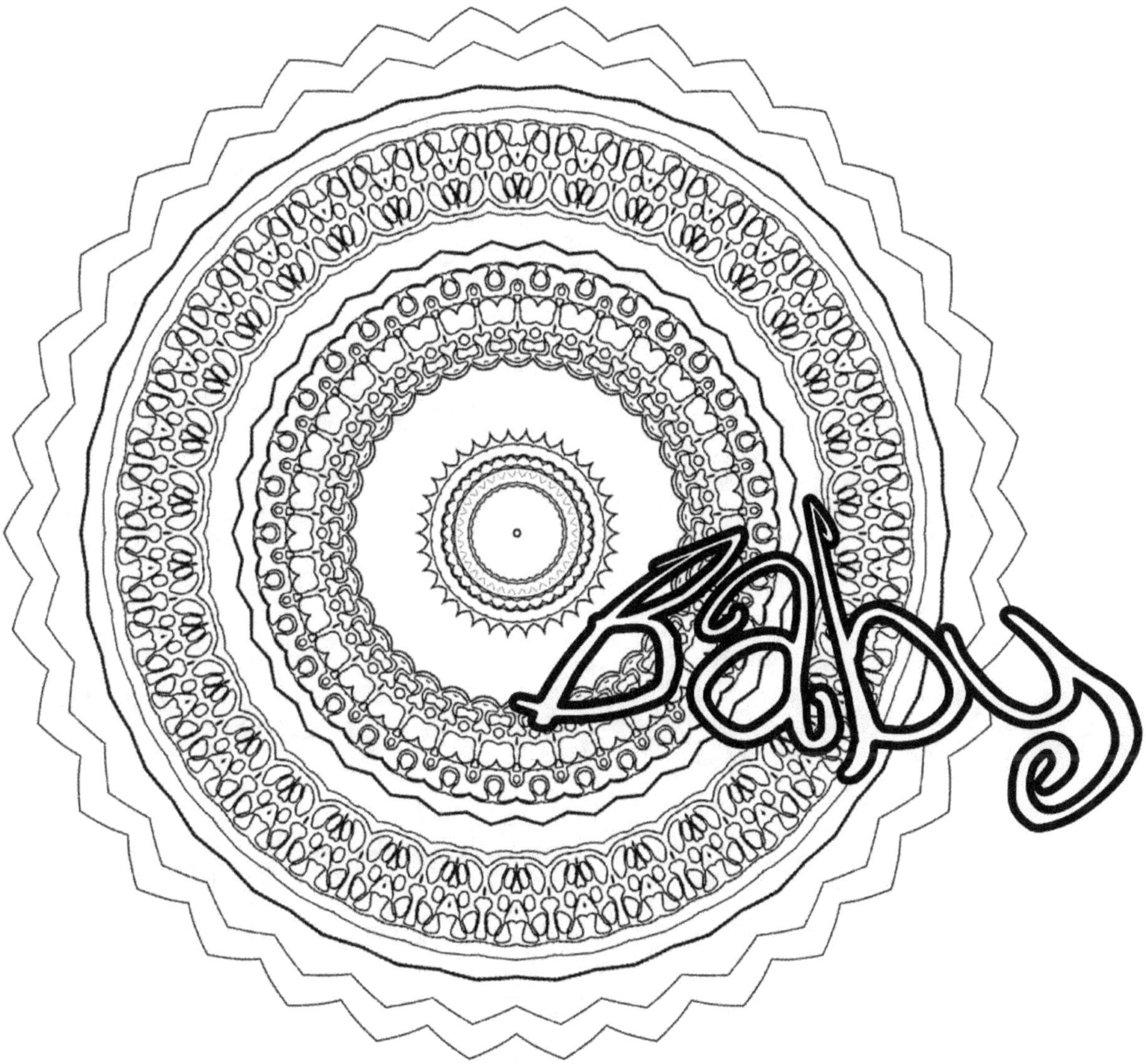
Baby

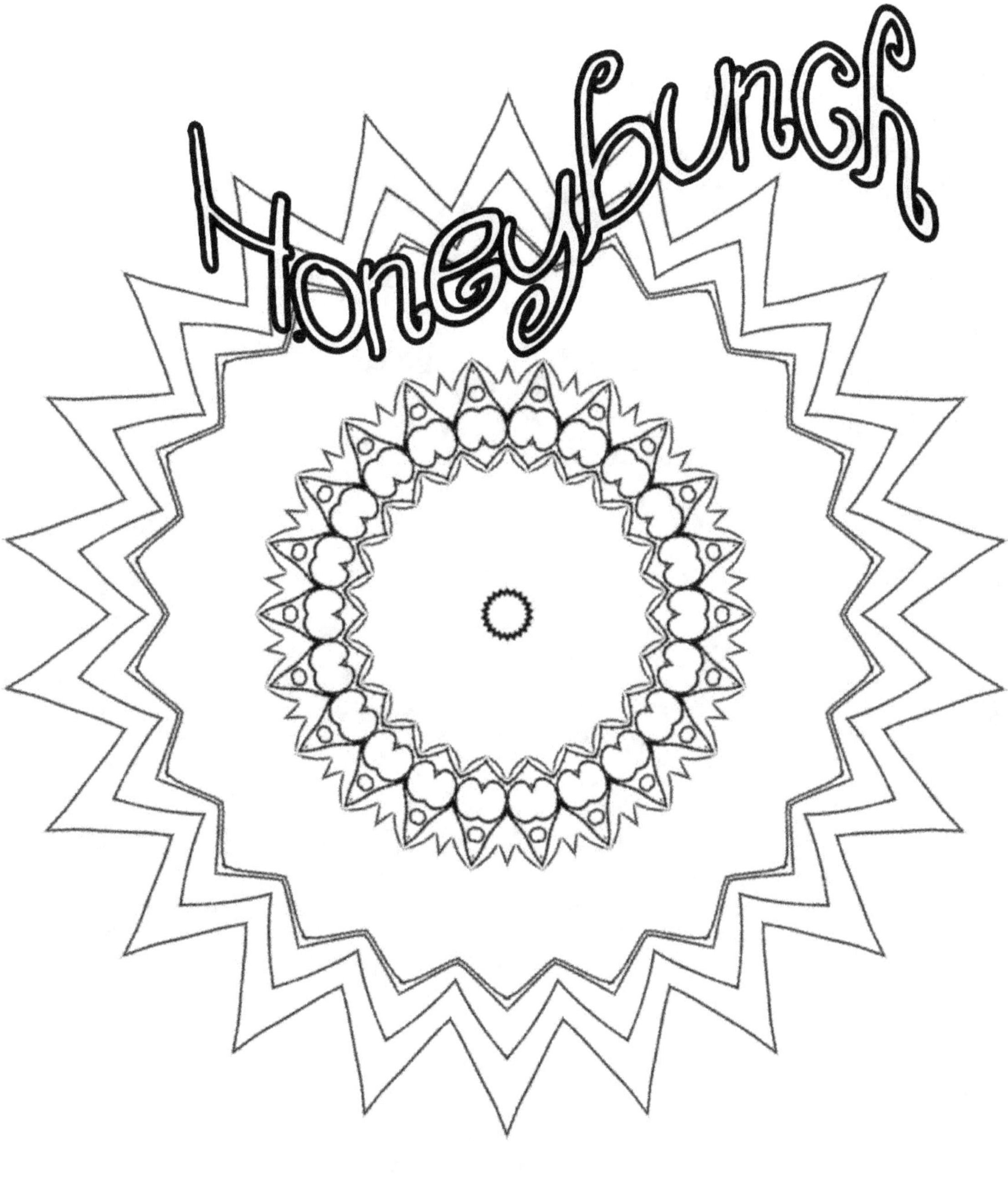
Honeybunch

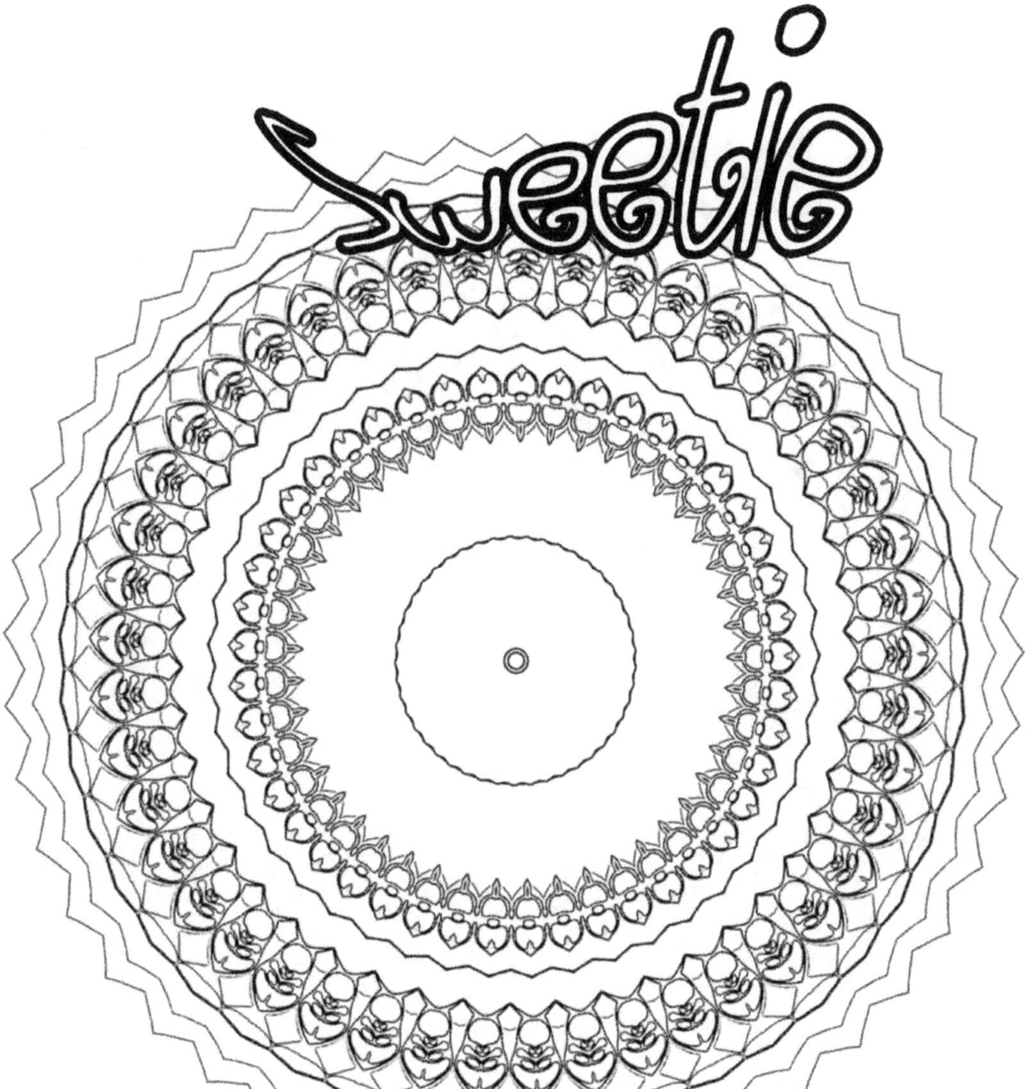
sweetie

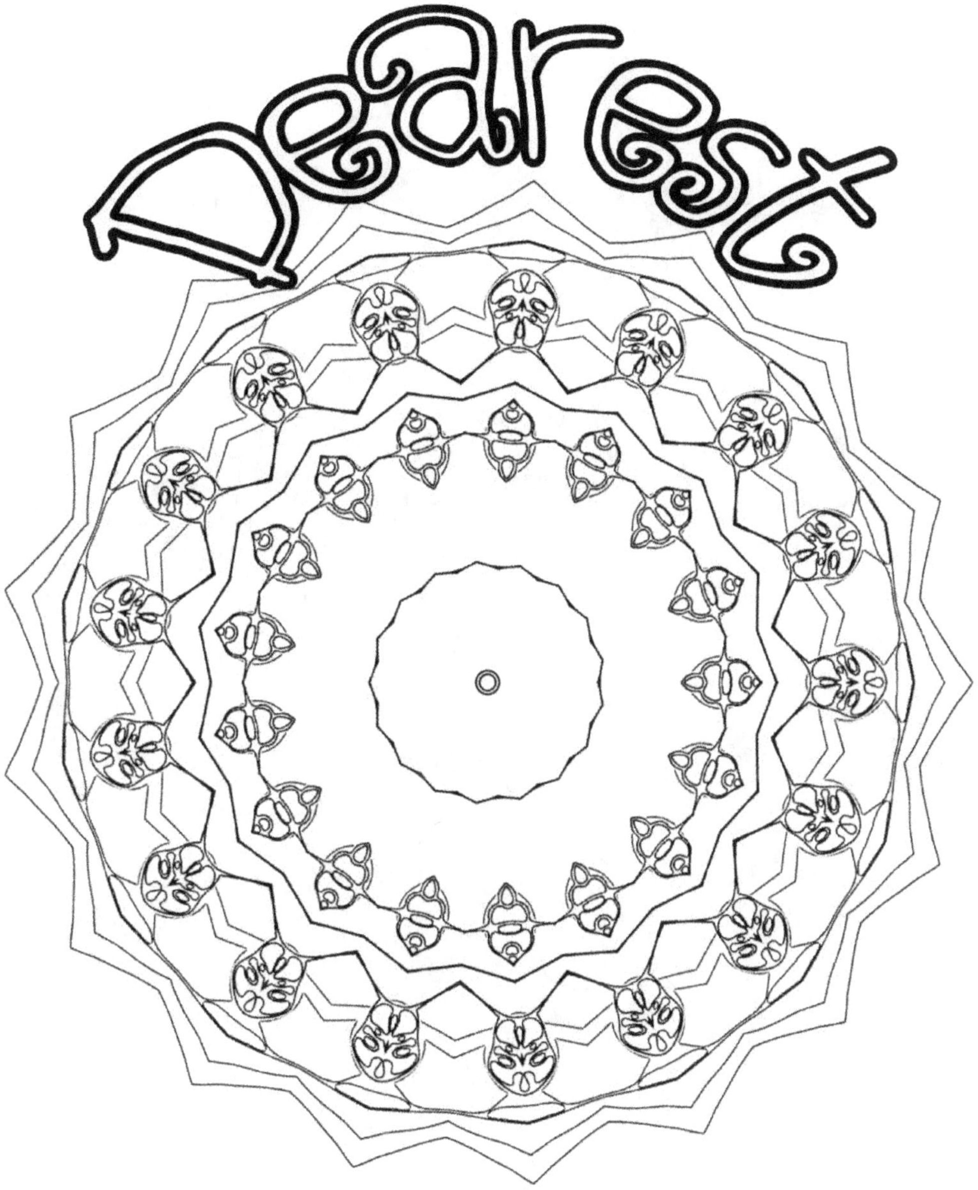
Dearest

My Beloved One

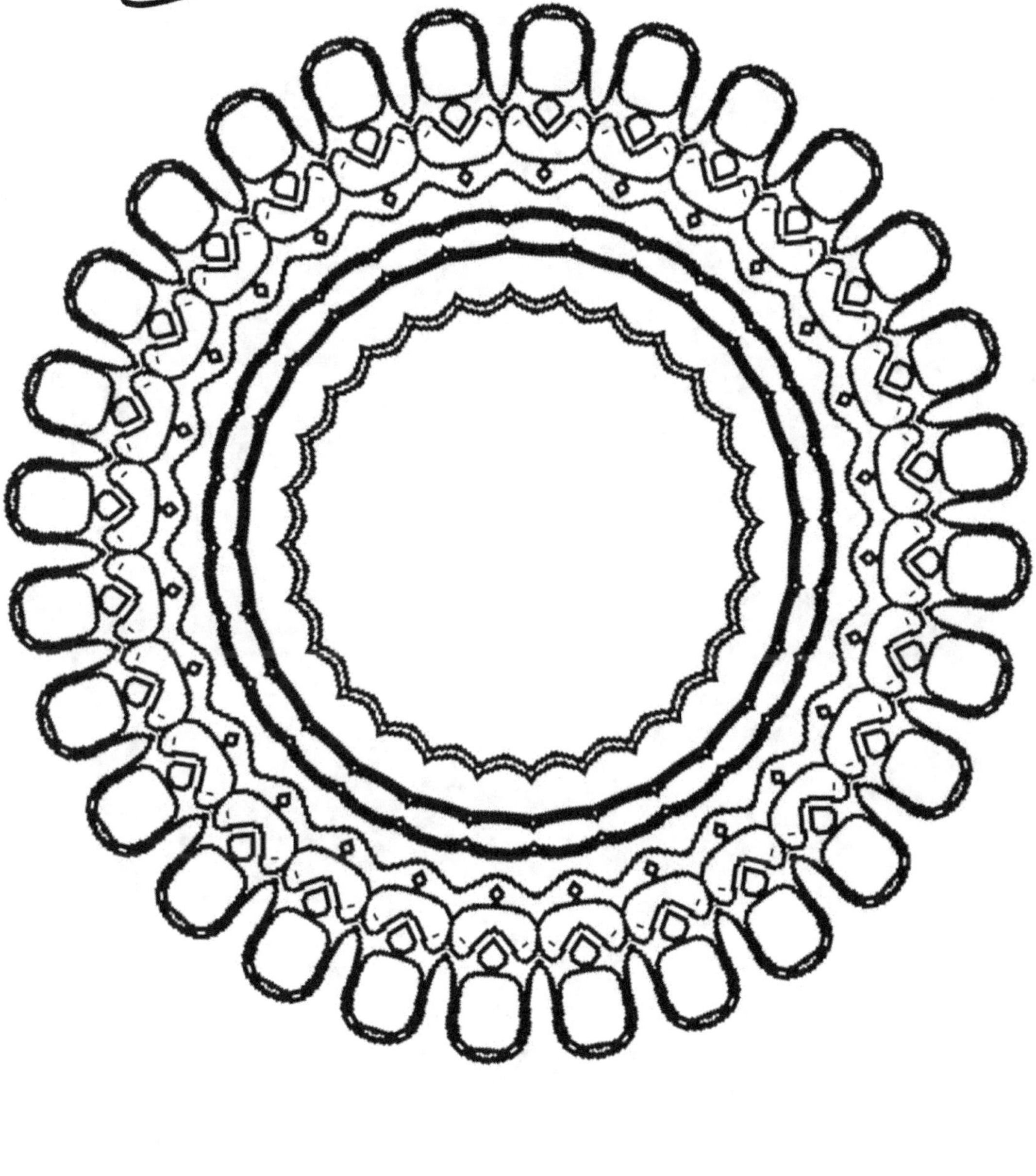

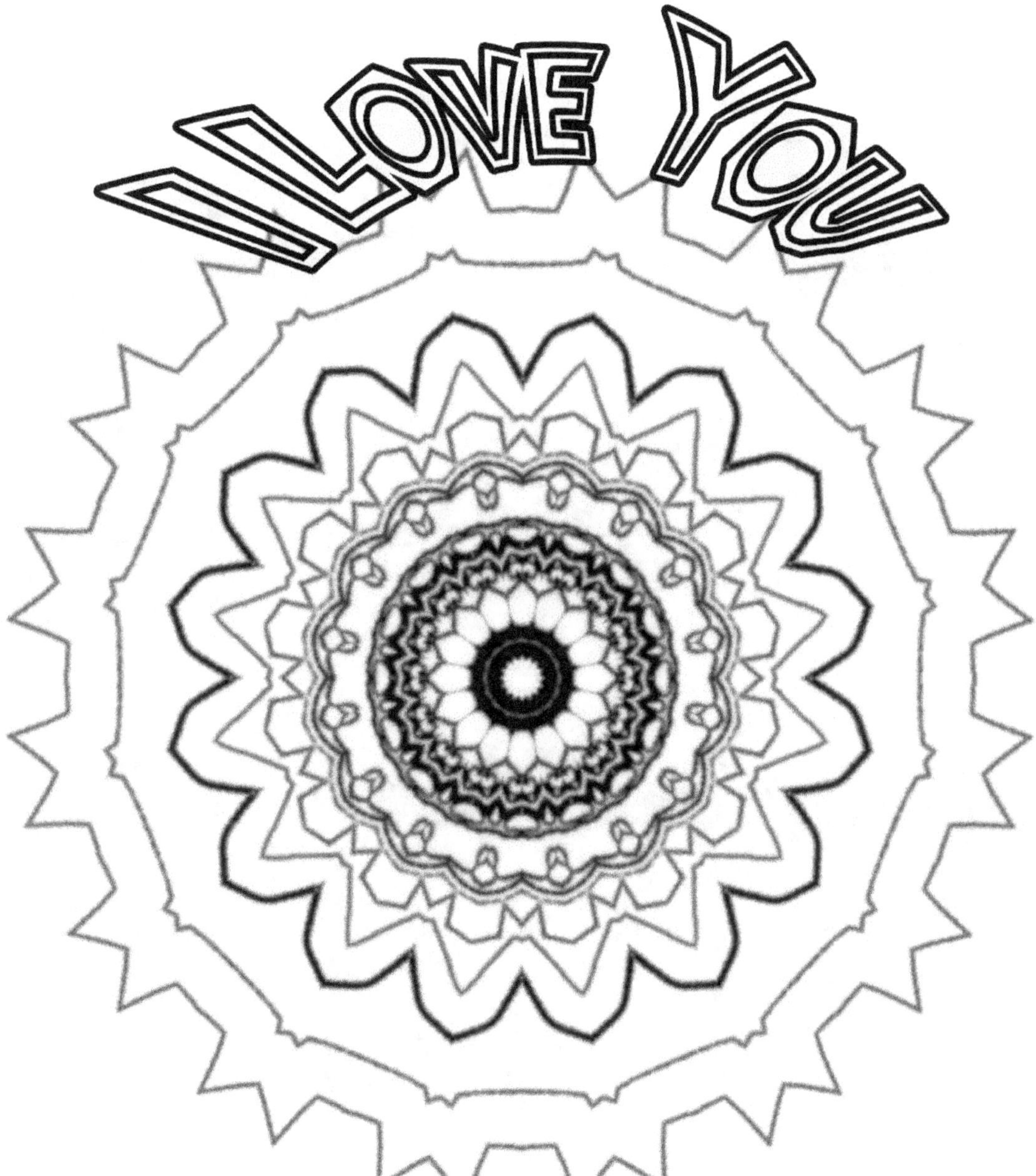
I LOVE YOU

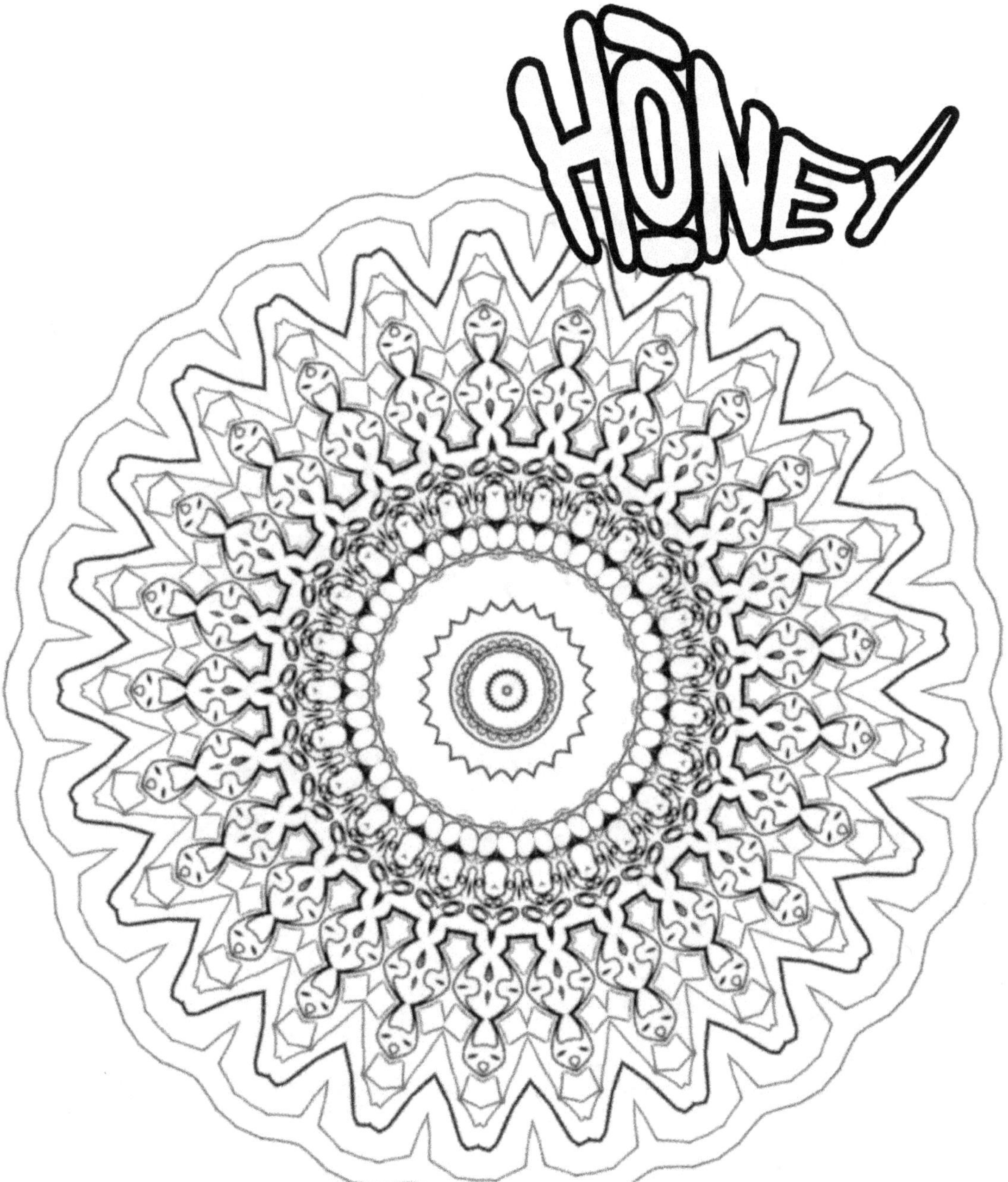
HONEY

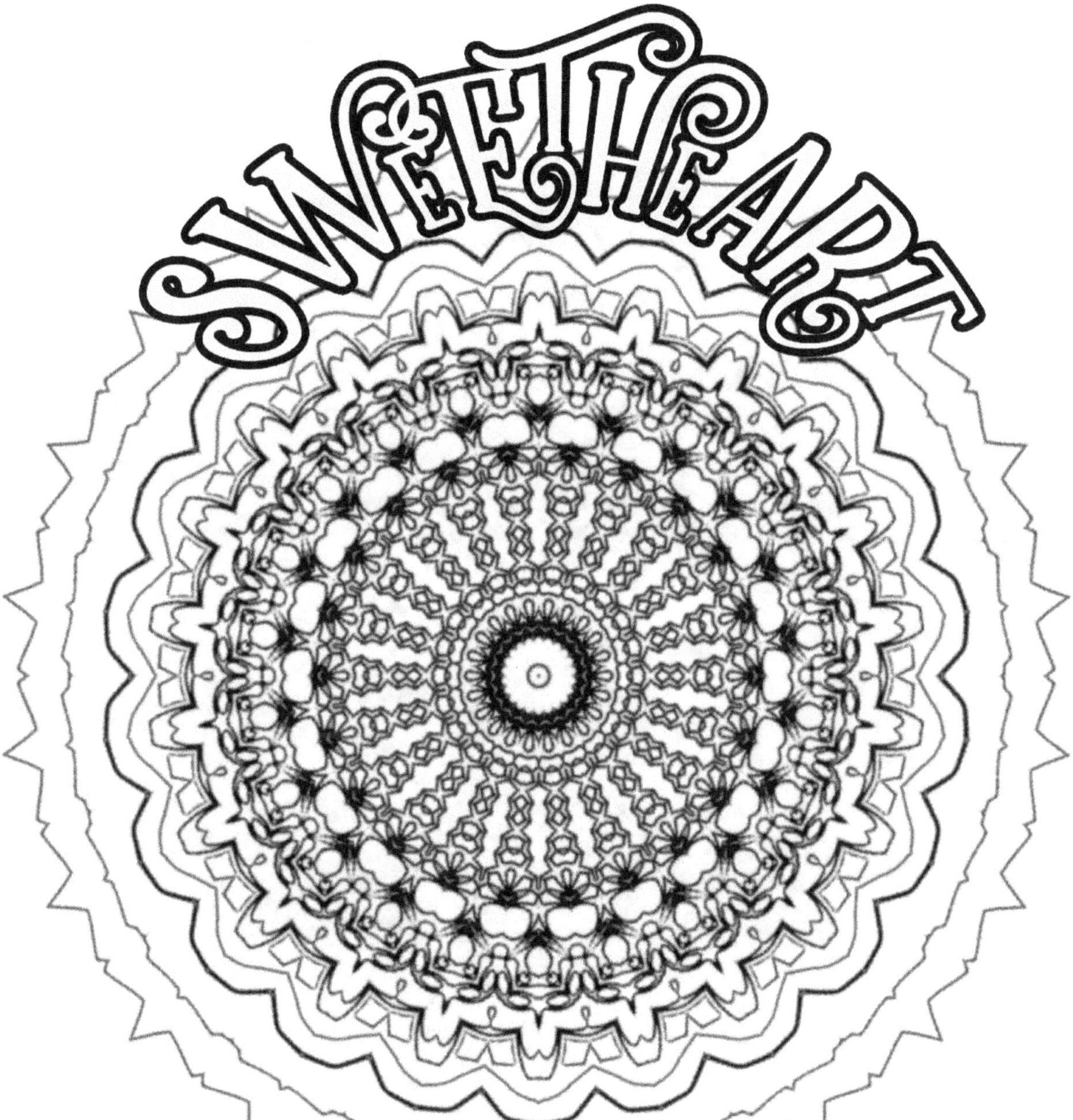
SWEETHEART

Darling

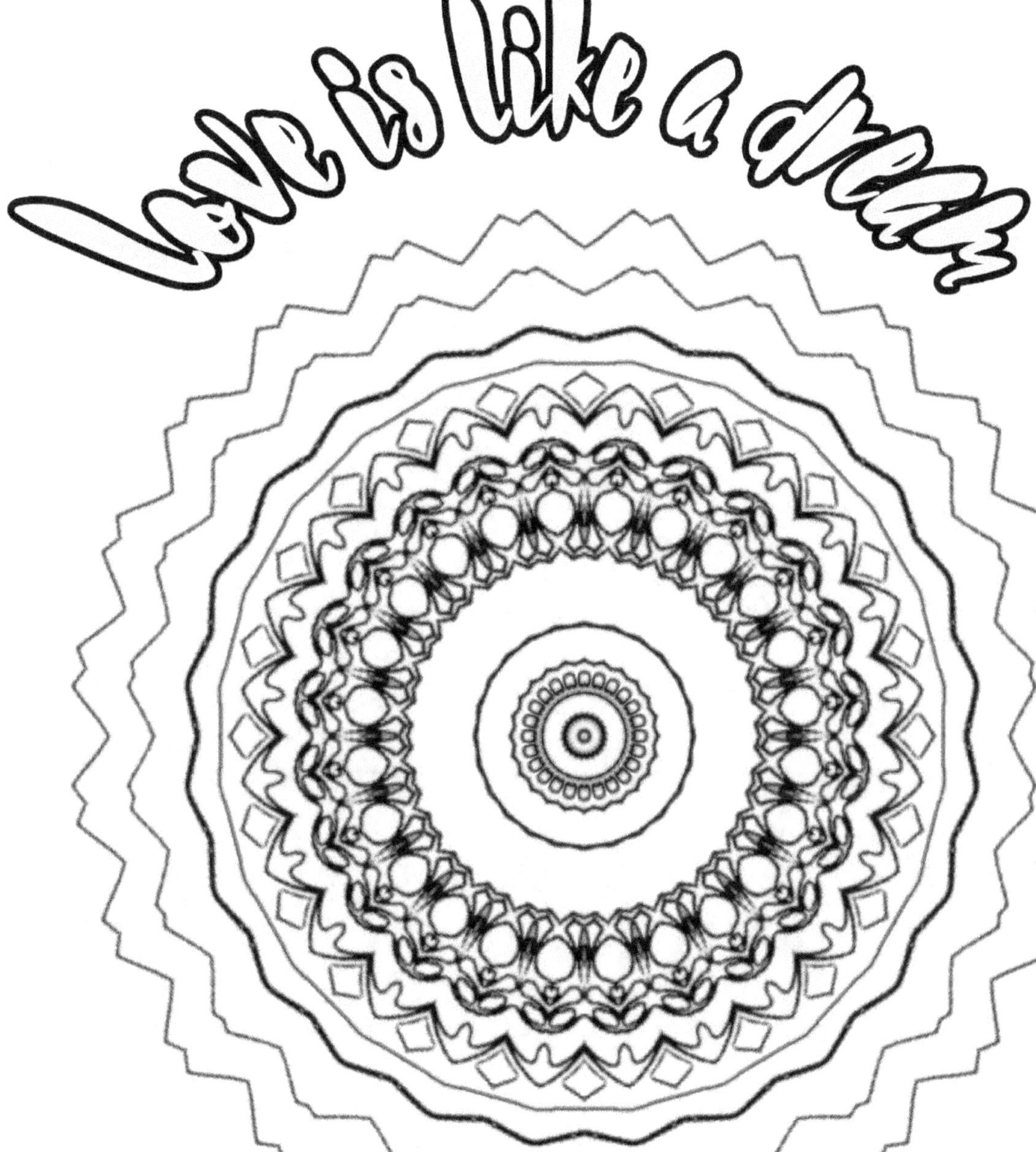
love is like a dream

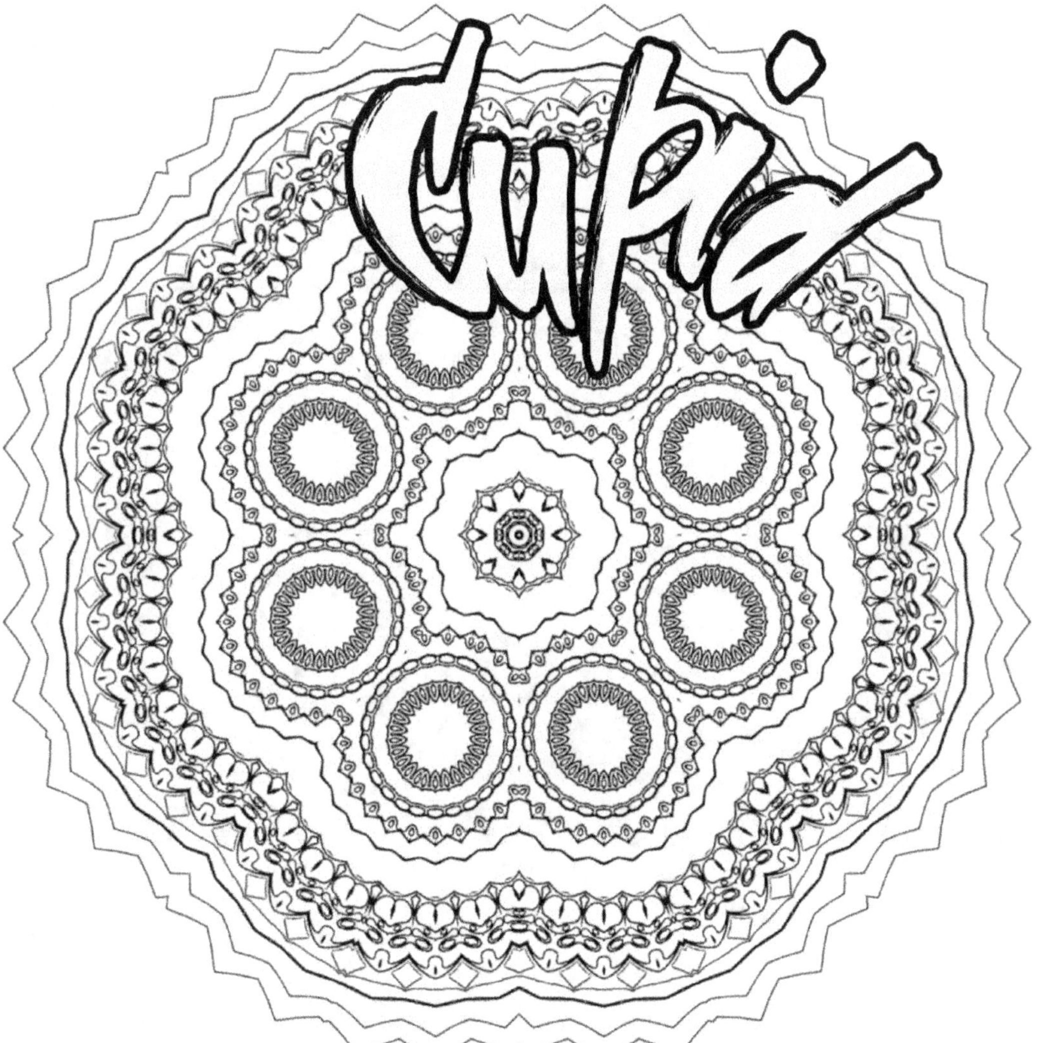
cupid

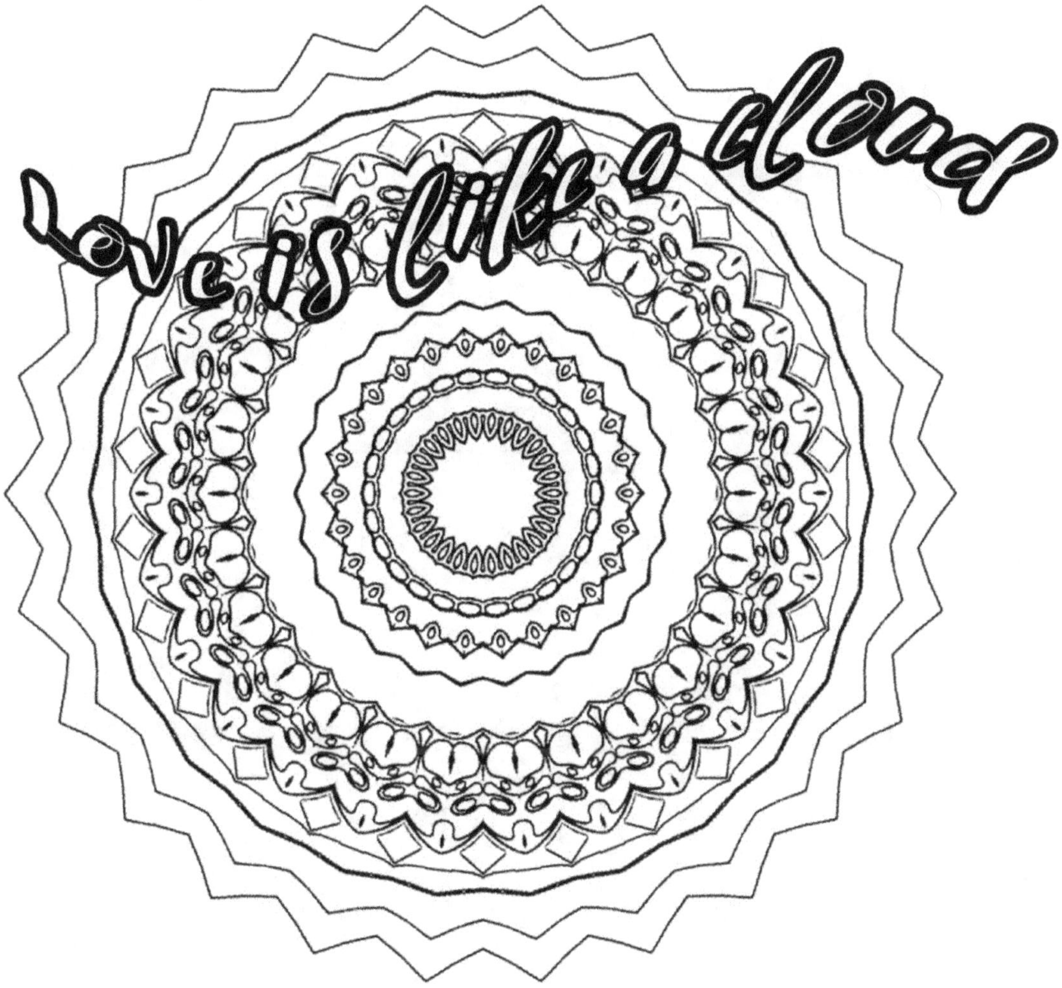
Love is like a cloud

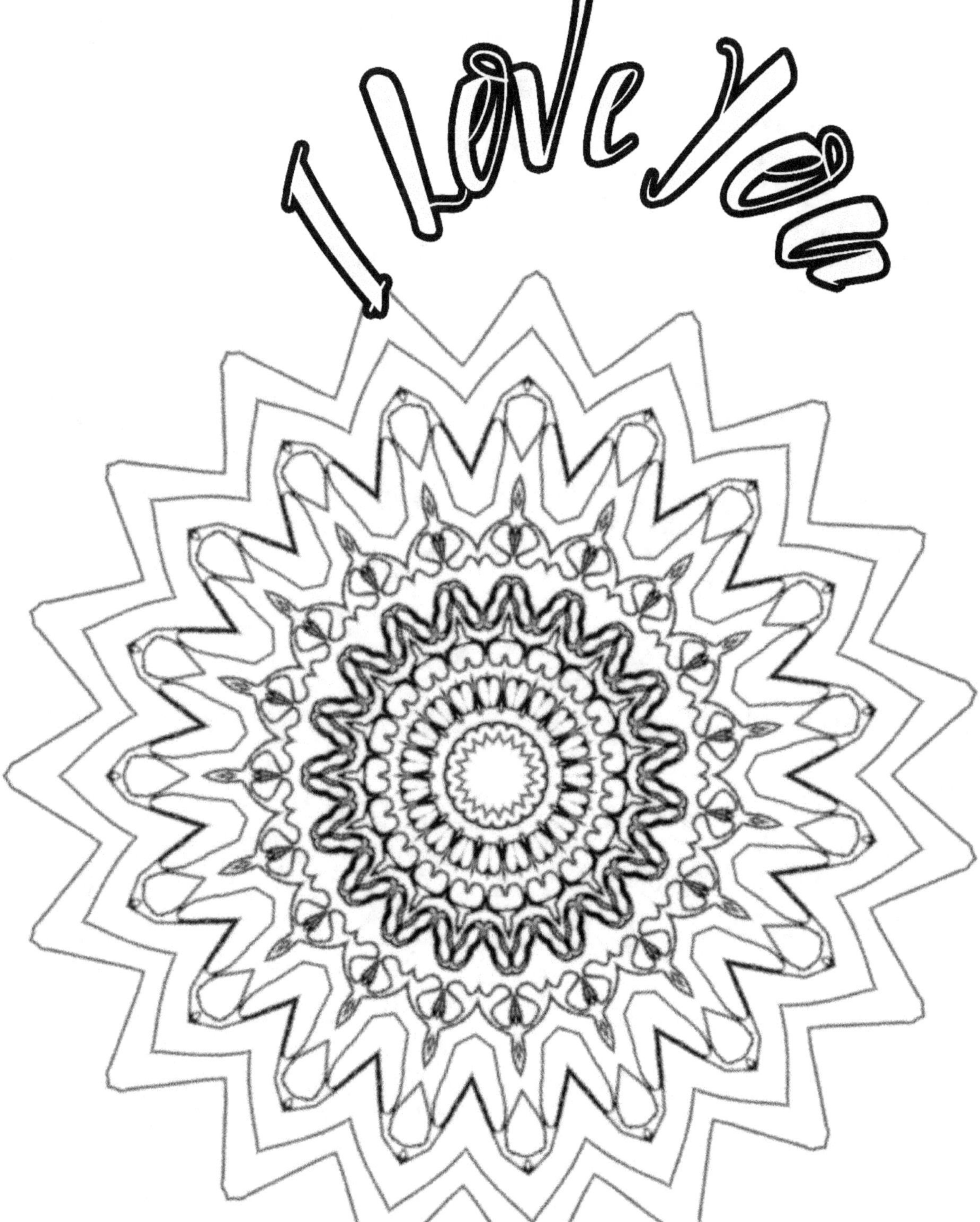
I Love You

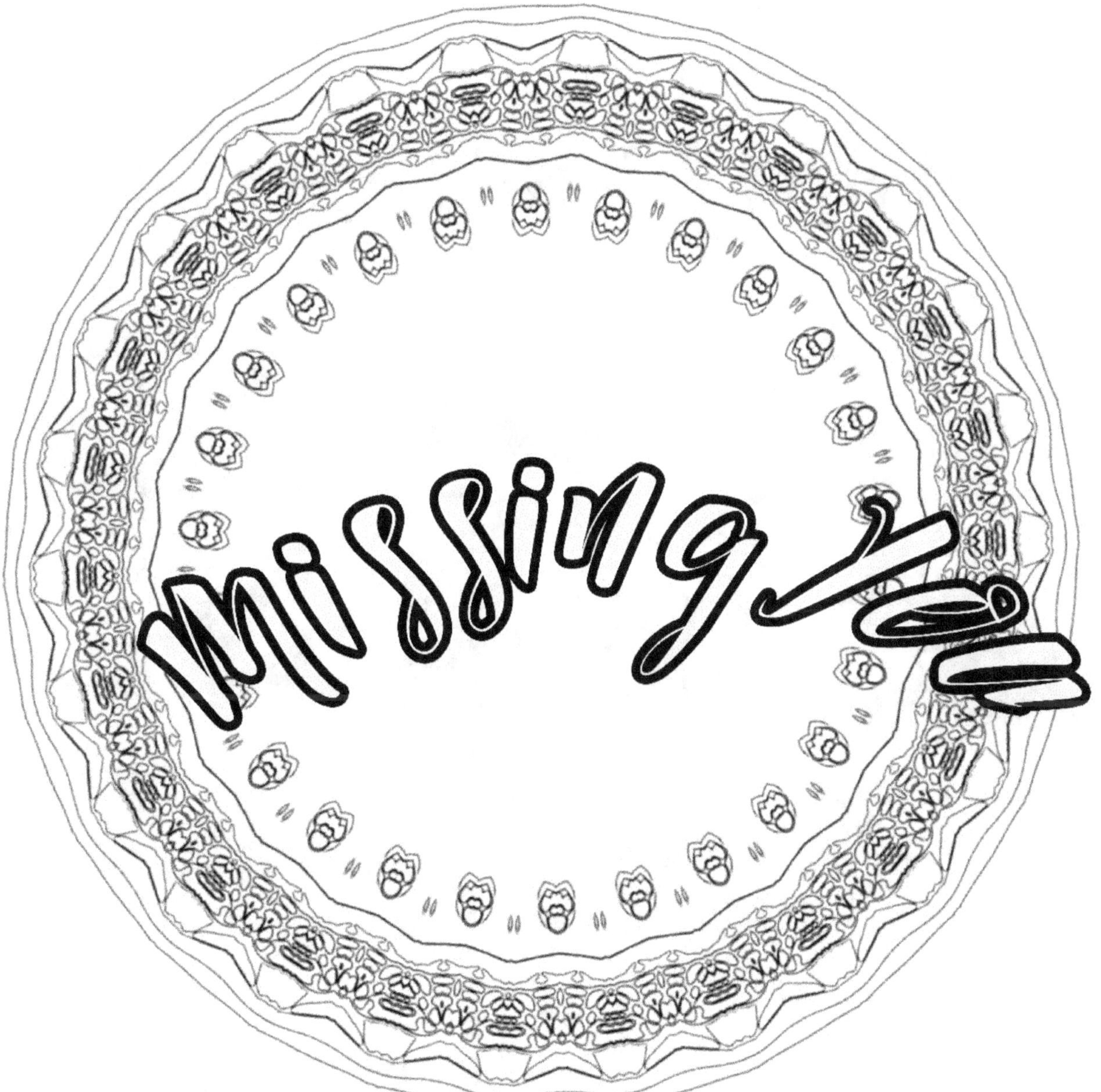
missing you

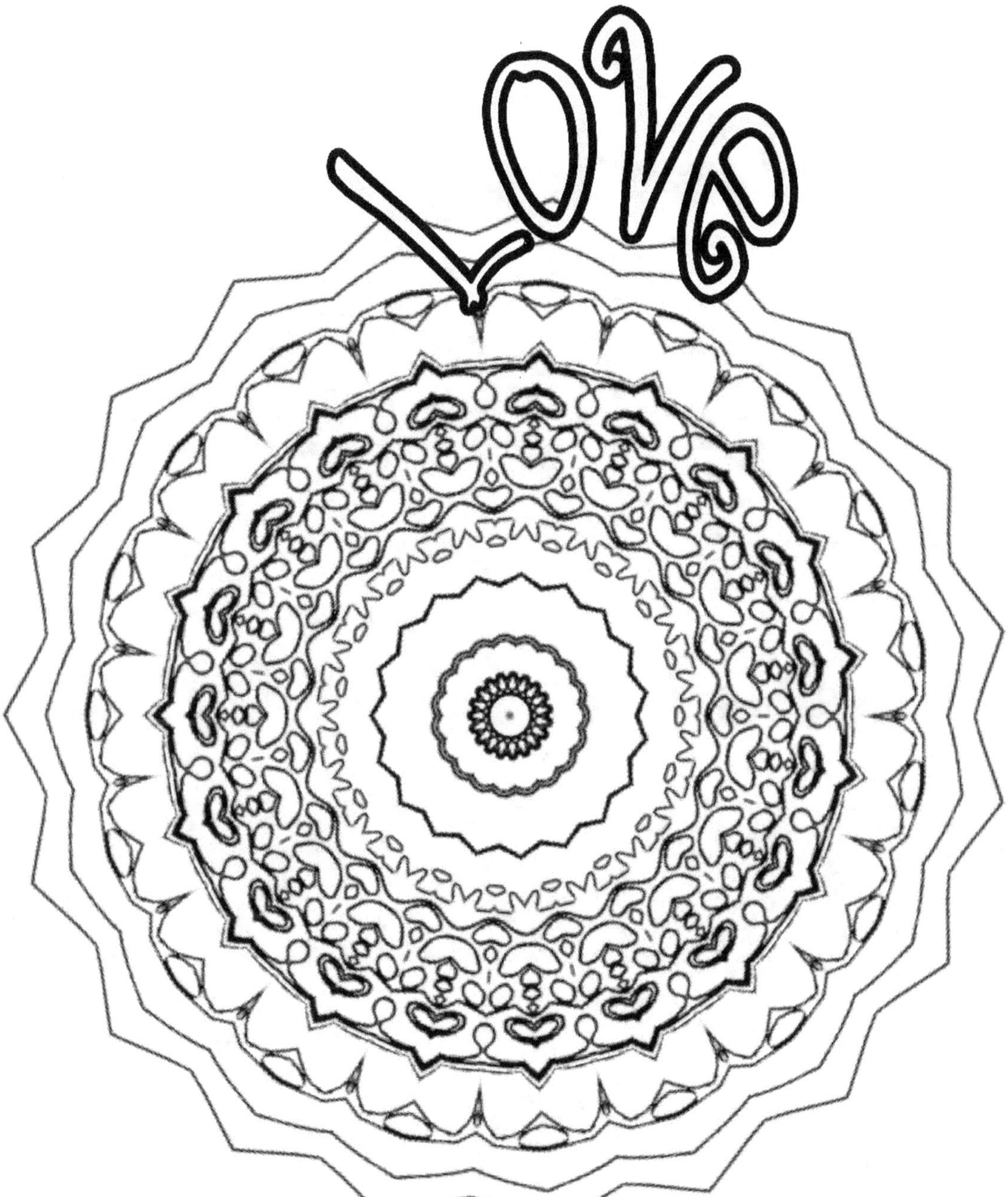
Love

www.ingramcontent.com/pod-product-compliance
Lightning Source LLC
Chambersburg PA
CBHW081751170526
45167CB00009B/3995
* 9 7 8 1 5 4 3 0 2 5 7 5 0 *